RECLAIM
YOURSELF

Rediscover your Power, Purpose & Magic

Learn and Un-learn until you Re-learn everything

ANISHA ROSHAL RODRIGUES

Reclaim Yourself

Publisher: Inkscribe Publishing Pvt. Ltd.

ISBN Number: 978-1-969259-89-0

Acknowledgement

I would like to dedicate this book to my family, friends, and loved ones, especially to Rhea Nicola Pinto & Daren Naren Miranda.

Preface

It was evening at about 4 pm when Daren came up to me and said, **"To be you costs nothing, but everything."** We were in school waiting for our buses to arrive to head back home while still listening to the nonchalant chatter of our friends, the noisy vehicles, and the children around us. It wasn't till my early twenties that I understood this phrase or even a part of it. It was like some sort of metaphysical theory that was beyond comprehension but still explicable. The minute I understood this phrase; I had a eureka moment and from that day I came to be known as **'WEIRDO'.**

Self-realization, although it is an intrinsic part of human nature, has almost become a difficult process for the masses to actualize. Now you must be wondering how it struck me. Well, grab a coffee and sit in the most comfortable place you could ever find right now, and let's move past the shore together.

Contents

Chapter 1

Absurdity

Every coin has two sides, but humans have many of them. The most amazing time one has is when they are young. The aura surrounding us in our youth is almost as vast as the entire universe. The amount of receptiveness and perceptions are equal to the collective consciousness of that of the cosmos, while the ego and rationalization process are significantly underdeveloped.

While I was about three or four, I remember my closest encounters with the spiritual world. I remember attending this funeral and seeing something like a cross catch up and go to heaven. The people around me were remorseful, while I was wondering what happened next to that cross and how it disappeared. Since then, a lot of my activity was absurd, like I would feel phantom touches, different people would talk to me, narrate different stories, and even comfort me at times. Emotionally I was very receptive, and I could easily decipher a person's intentions. Although my parents never noticed this kind of behavior, and it's only from my memory, I do remember my dad saying that I would talk to a stone and even feel bad that he's alone. Consequently, as I started going to school, I forgot about these memories, brushed them somewhere in my head, and forgot about them all. This didn't make me realize until late that I was special and was sent here on earth for a purpose. However, down the lane, I realized that I could indeed see through people, circumstances, and situations, and what had occurred previously was only a prologue of how my life would be in the future.

It was the afternoon of 2004 when I was in school one day, and I had to stay in the classroom since I didn't finish my work. The basic rule that I had to follow while writing numbers from 1 to 20 was that I had to leave a row in between and then move on to the next one similarly. I wouldn't understand the need of doing the same. When I did ask the reason, she simply told me that it would look neat. Not exaggerating the fact that she did have a point, but that is how I realized that society has its way of controlling your thoughts, ideas, emotions, and very being. The first-ever rule you would learn in a school is to **OBEY**. Even if you would try doing something that was not in the book, the teacher wouldn't give you the appropriate marks for using other methods that aren't prescribed in the book. Thus, it formed a pattern of compliance within our minds, and we started to lose originality.

Do you remember saying these things to yourself?

I'll not be welcomed if I do this.

What will people say about me?

I feel scared/nervous.

I'm not good enough.

I'm scared of being called a weirdo.

People will mock me.

Even if anything among these is true for you, do not be scared. Just remember that the world is filled with ordinary people, but you are extraordinary, so you feel out of place.

Exercises

If you feel any of these above emotions, congratulate yourself for belonging to the 10% club.

Take a deep breath and count to 3 and exhale it slowly and steadily. Repeat this process about as many times as you wish to until your mind is free of distractions.

Focus on a particular intention/question that you have regarding your uniqueness and ask the universe to answer it for you.

Realize that your absurdity stems from a purpose to benefit the collective humankind and set everything right.

Your absurdity is not something to be considered weird; rather, it contributes to your surreal nature.

Chapter 2

Acknowledgment

Now that you have understood what it takes to be different, let me take you toward the next step. It is undoubtedly acknowledging the fact that you are indeed different. Many of us don't take a lot of time to understand that we are different, but the lack of acknowledgement from our side makes it difficult for us to reach the ultimate state of self-realization. Acceptance in itself is an abundant gift that very few of us cherish. If we can learn to accept the small entities within or around us, we naturally awaken both our spiritual and subconscious states, which work wonders in no time.

Lack of self-acceptance can lead to decreased well-being and an overall decrease in other "self-related areas" as well. On the other hand, higher self-acceptance acts as a shield against negative experiences. Accepting yourself at an early stage doesn't require quite a lot of work. It just requires you to unconditionally accept yourself as who you truly are with all your flaws and limitations. We might feel overwhelmed by the energy we feel and absorb from ourselves as well as others, but that must simply be a reminder of the energetic, spiritual, and magnificent state that we possess so that we strive to love and accept ourselves as we truly are.

Exercises

Start with positive self-talk.

Use positive phrases at the start of the day and before you tuck yourself in bed. This will not only help you to change your perspective but will also change the neural programming of your brain.

Use **"I AM AFFIRMATIONS A LOT."**

Tell yourself the following every day:

1. I am AWESOME.
2. I am LOVED.
3. I am THE BEST.
4. I am PRECIOUS.
5. I am UNIQUE.
6. I am BEAUTIFUL.

Substitute with any word/quality you desire to possess and put "I AM" in front of it and see the magic for yourself.

Make this positive talk part of your everyday routine, and you will feel awesome. It takes an average of 66 days for a new behavior to become a habit. Therefore, if you practice it for one month, then you will do it automatically.

You can enhance this further by repeating all of these statements in front of the mirror.

If there is any behavior that you have issues dealing with, then just close your eyes and recall that behavior of yours and the way you respond to it. Once you have identified it, note it down and come to terms with yourself.

Forgive yourself. You are just another human with flaws, faults, and limitations. Don't be so hard on yourself. You deserve forgiveness.

Chapter 3

Forgiveness

Forgiveness is a virtue that only the strong have. All of us have the strength to forgive one another for our shortcomings. All that we need to realize is that all of us make mistakes, and that's okay. We are just mere humans, and it's okay not to be perfect at times. Our beauty lies in its imperfections. To practice forgiveness, we must first accept and acknowledge ourselves. Giving yourself permission is the most important step of the self-realization process, so make sure that you read and practice the first two steps well.

Lack of forgiveness makes us feel awful about ourselves and leads to feelings of remorse, guilt, grumpiness, incompleteness, and negative vibes in general. It makes us feel devoid of the good that we have and attracts a lot of negative energy. We can start small by doing little things like giving a smile to a person whom we dislike, greeting a random stranger, or even writing small notes to that particular person for whom it seems impossible to forgive.

Exercises

Count your blessings and name them one by one. Write down or say them aloud to make yourself feel pretty good all over again.

Meditate in silence and imagine in your mind the face of the person whom you cannot forgive. Recall the incident that incited these very feelings in you about that person. Now slowly and steadily feel your emotions. Visualize the conversation between you and that person. Feel his/her/their emotions.

Ask yourself these prominent questions:

a. What am I feeling?

b. What are they feeling?

c. Why did I start the fight?

d. What did they say back to me?

e. Was their or my point valid?

f. What prompted them to say the thing they were saying at that instant in time?

g. Did they have any negative experience in context with a particular person/situation?

h. How can I help them?

i. How can I help myself?

Once you've completed this process, take a notebook and draw an image of that entire experience. It will give you more insight than you could ever imagine.

Feel free to express your emotions either by crying, laughing, or even talking about it. Any emotion isn't bad to express. It's the living proof that you are a wonderful human. Express your emotions instead of keeping them bottled up. It's the best defense mechanism we could ever deploy, and your body will thank you for it.

Last but not least, go and hug that person, and they will talk to you. Trust in the fact that no human can ever resist a hug so filled with love and compassion because deep down that's all that we want. Don't bother to take this risk if that person exhibits mild to severe narcissistic traits. As much as others are important, so are you. Value your mental health more than people who don't value it. Of course, you can help them to get into a rehabilitation center and spend minimum time with them, but do not try this out if you're too sensitive and you simply cannot handle stress.

Chapter 4

Kindness

Kindness is the finest gift you could give to yourself and the whole world. Being kind is the next most positive thing you could do for yourself after those "I AM" statements. To learn this simple virtue, you have to do nothing but just be cheerful enough to do it. Kindness in itself is the godliest gift we could ever possess, and we should share it with others abundantly. After you're done with the earlier 3-step process to achieve self-realization, this is probably the easiest and most fun-loving step you could come in contact with. It's always a good idea to love, care for, and pamper yourself just a little more because no one will do that for you. Once you've freed yourselves from these shackles that had been controlling you so far, you must splurge on amazing things for yourselves too. It can be anything from a bubble bath to a trip to Hawaii because you deserve it. Always remember that you deserve to be **YOU!**

Your well-being includes your emotional, physical, and social health, and don't degrade it for anyone else. It's your right to be kind and to exhibit the same emotion toward your fellow beings as well.

Exercises

Talk to yourself aloud and say the following every day:

   a. I deserve kindness, and so do others.

   b. I am a magnet of kindness and generosity.

   c. I am kind.

Take a walk in a garden or go hiking.

Meet yourself in the depths of nature and be around lush greenery.

Do things that you loved doing as a little kid and evoke the childlikeness in you.

Meet random strangers and initiate a conversation with them.

Go on some adventurous trips.

Scream at the top of the mountain, "I LOVE ME."

Help the needy and comfort the distressed.

Visit people in the prison and tell them stories.

Spend a day at the orphanage.

Treat yourself to a solo movie trip with a bucketful of popcorn.

Chapter 5

Find Your Purpose

Now that you're an awesome person who's completely free of all the mess and who loves and understands themselves, it's time that you cherish the goodness present in you for a greater cause and a better good: serving both the almighty as well as humanity. That wonderful step that you would be taking next is called finding your purpose. All of us are given a mission and a goal to accomplish while we are on this planet, but not all of us realize it. Therefore, we need to get out of our preformed ideologies, systems, and beliefs and start questioning the events around us. We need to realize that the absolute way to find the answers to all our questions lies in asking them repetitively. It's crazy the way people have generalized, not asking questions and more of a follow-the-command behavior. It is crazy because they don't realize that in reality they're being controlled by many who do not want them to realize their true potential and power.

The trick is to not fall for the trap and instead start living out those very ideas you used to plan in your head in your own life. There is an ancient Japanese technique called **"IKIGAI"** that is used for the same.

Ikigai means a reason for being. It is a Japanese concept referring to having a direction or purpose in life, providing a sense of fulfillment to a person and towards which they may take actions, giving them satisfaction and a sense of meaning.

To discover your Ikigai, you must first find what you're most passionate about. Thereafter, you can find a medium to express that passion. However, there's a difference between important things in your life and your life's work. Ikigai is about finding joy, fulfillment, and balance in the daily routine of life. The fundamental truth of Ikigai is that everything is connected. Ikigai fosters the notion that you can be true to your passions, live a life of consequence, and still use your profession as a medium of expression.

Ask the following questions to find out your Ikigai:

What do you love doing?

What are you good at?

What does the world need?

What can you get paid for?

Let's deep dive into all of these aspects now.

You Love It.

What you love doing is usually easy to identify, as it pops up in your brain right away as someone talks about it. It was always something you most probably loved doing as a child, or even growing up, you would quite often do it. It can be anything from your hobbies to the skillset you possess. It could include an ocean of different things like drawing, painting, skating, playing, singing, dancing, theater, trekking, yoga, reading books, listening to music, playing your favorite instrument, and even talking to random strangers and connecting with them quite easily.

A few questions to ask yourself in this process:

What did you love doing as a child?

What are your current interests?

If you would combine the above two answers, what sort of a creative outcome could you derive from it?

Would this creative outcome act as a side job or would it give you that side cash you've been looking for, or are you feeling happy after starting this initiative?

How is this helping you to live your awesome life?

How are you contributing to a progressive society in general?

You're Good at It.

Now, this is pretty easy to identify, as you have already invested your energy into it and are progressing towards it efficiently. You can actively compete with someone if they were to do so concerning this talent that you're good at. You are probably a master in this topic, but you haven't identified the different areas, methods, and interests in which this would have benefitted you. If you have identified it, then probably you have just started with it, but don't worry because you are going on the right track. Keep progressing because persistence yields progress, which in turn yields success. If you feel that you are talentless and you're not good at anything, then you should probably stop thinking in that direction. Low self-esteem breeds extremely low self-confidence, which depletes success levels. Turn that pessimistic approach into an optimistic one. Focus on the bright side of life and start identifying your plus points. All of us have been blessed with various talents, but only some of us identify them. There is a saying in the Bible that says, *"For to everyone who has, more will be given, and he will have abundance; but from him who has not, even what he has will be taken away."* - *Matthew 25:29*

This simply explains the law of abundance. One who uses their gifts and potential will be given more, and the one who doesn't use their time and effort for the same will have it taken away from them. The universe rewards the one who puts in all their effort and energy to consciously evolve the universe along with themselves and not the one who wastes his energy. If you ever feel that your life has reached a standstill, then it is probably because you've never corresponded with the universe.

To-Do List

Realize your potential.

Ask questions.

Believe in yourself.

Show gratitude exclusively.

Do something good for Mother Nature.

Take small steps in being considerate towards others.

Take baby steps towards developing your interest.

The World Needs You.

Yes, you read it right. The world indeed needs you a lot. You're the hope this desperate world needs. You're that ray of sunshine that people encounter at the end of the tunnel. Therefore, do not pay heed to anyone who says that you are unimportant, unworthy, and incapable of changing the world because at your core and in your truest potential, you are a revolutionary. I spoke a lot about trusting, believing, and understanding yourself. Now let us talk about giving back to society. Till this point whatever you did was only to improvise and make yourself better, but from now on you will focus on these very things to make the world better both for you and the entire human race. The littlest of the deeds you do to a living being brings about drastic changes in the overall positive energies all around the world. This happens because of magic that connects us all, called **LOVE.** Therefore, do not underestimate your capacity to contribute to society. It can provide monetary, social service, educational, or entertaining value. Whatever you feel the world needs is exactly what it needs. Don't doubt your intuition. You can create magic with it. Just remember one thing: when you give something to the world, you get back more than you expect. So don't stop this cycle no matter what because goodness repays goodness and yields godliness.

Give without expecting anything in return, for that's the most beautiful universal law.

You Get Paid for It.

This is what you are currently doing or what you aspire to do for the rest of your life. For most of us, it is a stable job that feeds our family, fulfills our needs, gives us a comfortable life, and helps us to maintain a status in our society. This either makes us feel good about ourselves, or we're doing it because we don't have a choice. If you agreed with the latter option, then maybe you never realized what upskilling could ever do to you. If you're stuck at a day job and you want to push your limits but you feel like you don't have a way out, then maybe you should start researching more often. Research new job opportunities, new skills that you could learn, newer ways to generate profits, and even better ways to make yourself satisfied. You can never learn too much and know too little because till the end of our time we remain students, while still teaching others.

Tips and Tricks

Be eager and ready to learn new things every day.

Don't just learn it; do it instead.

Always have a mentor to guide you.

Do it the fun way.

Travel and explore more. You don't always need to travel to exclusive foreign locations. Try traveling to the interior villages, different towns, and cities and learn a thing or two.

Don't be society dependent; be independent in your thinking.

Finally, get some work done. Don't plan it in your head a lot; start executing already.

When you start doing it, you're already halfway there.

Chapter 6

Live and Help Others Find their Purpose

Once you have realized and are living your purpose, help others find it as well. A single person can inspire millions, but the power of millions inspiring millions would evolve our whole human civilization. You might have faced a difficult journey on your path to your purpose, but you have learned your lessons, you've had your share of hardships, and you're on your way to understanding and creating your reality. You might not be able to walk your friend's path or even have a share in their journey, but all that you can do is share and explain to them your experience so that they will be mentally and physically ready to take up this challenge. All of us have our own very distinct paths to attain self-realization, and none can imitate others' paths because if they were to do so, it would be very difficult for them.

To-Do List

Talk about your experience with your friend.

Refer him/her/them to this book.

Prepare them mentally for this emotional rollercoaster ride.

Explain to them the pros and cons of this journey.

Be their helper when it's difficult for them in their journey.

Ask them if they need help.

Be approachable to them.

Have a goal in mind while helping others. For example, I want to help ten of my friends to achieve their purpose in life, and in return they must help ten other people as well.

Help and don't expect anything in return.

Start a small Facebook or Telegram group wherein different people could pitch in their ideas and suggestions relating to this topic.

Have small gatherings at a club, or start your club and meet each other in person.

Get more people to join you and make small contributions from your side occasionally.

Chapter 7

Explore the World

Up till now what you did on a smaller scale, extend it up to a larger scale and spread the word to all parts of the world. Travel more often and meet people from different walks of life. Listen to their stories and tell them yours as well. If you have started anything like a small group or an organization, reach out to them, explain to them, and help them create a mini replica of what you've already been doing. The world will love you even more if you can adapt, adjust, and accept their culture. People will start liking you in general, and your ideas, knowledge, expertise, and brand will be more acceptable to them only because you have made them feel that their way of living is awesome and you like it too. Always follow these guidelines if you're traveling abroad.

Do's

Beware of your surroundings.

Only carry as much cash as is needed.

Lock up valuables.

Memorize your passport number. You should have a copy of your passport stored in another location. If it becomes lost/stolen, knowing your number will speed up the replacement.

Memorize your credit card number and important phone numbers to call in case your card is lost or stolen. Make copies and leave a list at home.

Follow the buddy system. Always travel with a friend/group.

Have loads of fun!

Don'ts

Carry and publicly show large amounts of money or exchange currency at places that do not appear safe and secure.

Walk with a purse or bag loosely over one shoulder. Instead, carry a backpack and keep it on your chest.

Go to places not listed on your itinerary, and you will learn more.

Use your phone a lot, and you'll miss the fun parts.

Chapter 8

Relationships

*"Too often we underestimate the power of a touch,
a smile, a kind word, a listening ear, an honest compliment
or the smallest act of caring, all of which have the
potential to turn a life around."*
– Leo Buscaglia

Relationships are the most integral part of our lives. We love and care for the people around us. All of our relationships in life nurture various qualities and aspects within us. It changes our outlook on our lives and impacts us in several ways. It is a force stronger than gravity itself that holds everyone and everything together. It is a mighty weapon that everyone has for their benefit. Relationships, like the strongest ships, remain unaffected by the strongest winds, yet a small iceberg can devastate them. It is very essential to nurture and take care of them as you would a plant. Relationships can be of different kinds, such as the ones you have with your family, friends, potential partners, professional acquaintances, and the one with yourself. Most of us fulfill our duties in all the other aspects other than the self, and that's the reason this book exists. To make you feel that you're not alone in this journey and that it's okay to be selfish and take care of yourself. You deserve your break and space, too.

Let's discuss all of these in detail now.

You Love Yourself

You are your first love. You are your foremost priority. You are the most important person to yourself. If you felt bad while reading these sentences or you slightly negated these statements, stating that others are more important than you are, then you need to rethink the amount of time you give yourself. It's your moral duty to take care of and nourish yourself because nobody will do that for you. It is not appropriate of you to expect others to take care of you. The mess you created shall be set free by you yourself. Others can guide you on how you can go about self-love, but the initiative has to be taken by you. Every mess in all its brokenness contains an adventure, a lesson, and a polish, all of which are required to carve you out super beautifully.

Self-love makes us believe in ourselves, our abilities, and our talents and helps us deal with ourselves sweetly. It helps us to manage ourselves in the most desperate situations as well. Therefore, an important part of always being an enlightened human being is to love yourself dearly.

Exercises

Incorporate a generous amount of "**DEARS**" for yourself each day. Use phrases such as "I love you, dearest," "Dear (your name), you are awesome," etc.

Start practicing yoga and meditation every day. Thirty minutes of meditation can attract loads of opportunities and peace of mind to your life.

Have a routine and stick to it. Keep at least an hour for yourself every day.

Have a morning routine. Start your day with a mindful meditation followed by yoga every day.

Don't look at your phone early in the morning.

Have a night routine. Review your entire day and go about it, acknowledge your flaws, and decide upon certain behaviors you might want to change.

Vent out to yourself every day about anyone whose behavior you didn't find appropriate, that sadistic person, that gloomy girl, or anything that happened that day with yourself.

Talk to your body and ask how it is feeling. There will be a soft voice that will tell you the answer. It's called intuition; trust it.

You are undoubtedly messy, and so you should be because none of us are perfect, but do remember to hug yourself once you're done crying.

Treat yourself to the smell of some flowers or even some candles as well.

Start journaling and be consistent.

Switch to a more balanced diet. Curate a diet plan that would consist of 5 days of eating vegetarian and 2 days of eating non-vegetarian foods.

You Love Your Family

"Family is one of nature's masterpieces."
– George Santayana

Family is indeed the best group of people whom you could ever rely on during your worst times. It is a blessing from the almighty to have a wonderful loving family. Our basic family comprises our parents, siblings, grandparents, and our closest uncles and aunts. They act as our support system and are there to help and inspire us in our difficult times. Families are supposed to nurture and help us be good citizens with moral values. Your family should be your go-to for everything. Your family loves you more than you could ever think and will be there for you no matter what.

If you feel that you've had a terrible experience with your immediate family members, then please don't lose your heart. You happened to cross paths with the wrong people during a pivotal phase in your life. I want to remind you that you still have hope and there are people out there who care for you. Get up, wash your face, and make a firm decision about your life and your next steps. There are people out there who've made it literally through nothing, and so will you. You are an embodiment of grace, love, and awesomeness. Show that to the world, and there will be people who will love and support you. Initially, it might be painful, but trust me, you will get through this too.

If you could resonate with either the good or the bad version of family, there are things you can do to improvise the current status quo with the people you love the most.

Talk to your family members more often. Talk to them about the way you feel about them and express genuine concerns that you think might affect your relationship with them.

Prepare them for the conversation you're about to have with them.

Ask them to make some adjustments, and you make some yourself too.

Practice love and compassion towards your loved ones regularly.

Use encouraging statements like,

a. Thank you for behaving ----------(politely, gently, calmly)

b. You are doing a great job.

c. Thank you for doing this. You are an amazing friend/sister/ mother (or any other relationship).

d. I exude positive energy, love, peace, and harmony to you (name any person you would like to).

e. I forgive you as much as I forgive myself.

f.   You are loved, cared for, and wanted.

g.   You are important, dear, and near to me.

Practice these things for quite a long time, and don't let go of them until they become a part of your personality and theirs as well. Always remember this one thing: *"When you help someone else come out of their mess, you unfold yours as well."*

Always care for strangers because once upon a time your loved ones were also strangers, and they welcomed you wholeheartedly.

Last but not least, remember that gratitude and kindness never go out of fashion. It's the best gift we can give to ourselves as well as the world.

Chapter 9

Grief Management

"Grief is that sword that once pierced leaves a scourging pain on a wounded heart."
Anisha Rodrigues, aka me, the author

Grief is a distinctive feeling that encompasses just a lot more than sadness, emptiness, and pain. It is an emotional, ever-tangled mess that is hard to accept and come out from. We need to most importantly acknowledge the very feeling that grief is and accept it as it is. The most important thing about dealing with grief, though, is that we should accept that it's just another emotion that exists within our human society. It's okay to go through a rough patch, to feel intrinsic sadness, guilt, and remorse that will finally lead up to grief. We need to remember that at the end of the day, all our emotions exist for a reason, and all of them help us to cope with various life scenarios. Just make sure that you aren't overwhelmed a lot by grief and express your grief with a trusted person.

Exercises

Vent your heart out to your closest friend/relative.

Cry out as much as you can and empty the feeling of grief.

Journal your feelings if that's comfortable for you.

Seek help from a therapist or a counselor to help you to deal with it.

Try doing some quick exercises to keep you deviated from the negativity you're feeling.

Start venting out and talking to yourself rather than overplaying the entire incident in your head.

Express your grief in the manner you would like it. For example, sing a song, make a painting, record yourself, make a podcast, write it down, etc.

Get over the situation/incident already.

Remember that people, places, and properties are always temporary and not permanent.

To-Do List

Start with positive affirmations and kind sentences every day.

Hug yourself whenever you need one.

Talk to your mom. She has the best advice.

Always make sure to spend enough quality time with your loved ones no matter how bad/tiring your day was.

Take a good old nature walk or a trip somewhere to get it all off your chest.

Give yourself a second chance. You deserve that for existing on this planet.

Chapter 10

Eating Concerns

All of us love food! Isn't it? The basic thing is, why shouldn't we? After all, that's what all our mammalian instincts are like, and to fill one's hunger, one is ready to do anything that might come in one's way. Above all, one must really consider two aspects about food: one is having an excess of it, and the other is having an insufficiency of it. Both of these aspects aren't good for anyone and cause more damage to overall health than any other bodily aspect does. Let me get into both of these aspects in detail and explain everything step by step.

1. Overeating

Overeating is basically an eating disorder caused by excess eating due to the individual's discretion and lifestyle. This behavior often serves various purposes, such as compensating for a specific nutritional deficiency, filling a void in life, seeking validation, relieving stress and anxiety, and providing happiness and contentment when other sources of validation are lacking. Food is always known to impart comfort and give us validation that we like and deserve. In certain difficult situations, one must always remember other ways to seek comfort instead of overeating, as the ill effects of overeating take a lot of time to diminish. Some of the adverse effects of overeating include sluggishness, sleepiness, indigestion, increased risk of heart disease and cancer, obesity, insulin resistance, fatty liver, and decreased brain function. Overeating isn't the solution to any of your problems. If it's a habit that's hard to break, seek help from a professional, but don't give in to it so easily.

To-Do List

Regulate the amount of food intake that you consume every day.

Food intake and the number of calories every person needs differ anywhere from about 1,700 to 2,800 calories.

Drink plenty of fluids as well to regulate your solid food content.

Make a food schedule and stick to it.

Take the help of a nutritionist and follow a diet plan.

Don't rely on junk food, processed food items, and sugary drinks.

Make sure to always eat a balanced diet consisting of whole foods, grains, vegetables, fruits, fiber, etc.

Keep an accountability partner to help you stay on track with your food intake.

2. Malnutrition

Malnutrition is yet another eating disorder that affects about 462 million people worldwide. This health crisis is caused by a variety of reasons, like poor socioeconomic status, unequal distribution of food supplies, alcoholism and drugs, and other eating disorders like anorexia nervosa and bulimia. It is therefore just as bad as or worse than overeating and leads to an array of adverse effects. Some of the ill effects of malnutrition include reduced muscle and tissue mass, muscle wasting, decreased stamina, increased risk of chest infections, slower immune response, and poor libido and fertility problems. In such cases, professional help must be sought after to solve a major part of the problem.

To-Do List

Visit a good nutritionist and seek help immediately.

Follow the meal care plan strictly and make sure not to deviate from it.

Make sure to join in and be an active part of support groups, charity, and volunteering organizations.

Be an accountability partner for someone else suffering from a similar problem and help each other overcome the respective problem as well.

Chapter 11

Taming the Brain

We are all very susceptible to various mental and psychological diseases in our daily lives, as our life scenarios keep on changing, and so do our coping mechanisms. We develop such conditions over a long period of time. Worry not because all of these problems are faced by the majority, and there's both treatment and help that exists for these diseases. Let's open up and understand anxiety and depression in general and get to know how to cope with them better.

Anxiety

"Anxiety" is quite a normal term used for several dysfunctions that manifest as nervousness, apprehension, worry, and fear that mostly result from an uncertain event or a result and maybe due to a past experience as well. Anxiety is quite normal in most people but is deemed dangerous when it affects your sleep cycle and cognitive ability. Every person has different coping mechanisms in relation to anxiety. Each and every person deals with anxiety differently depending on their type, whether they're an empath or a narcissist. Either way, it's good to seek help in a timely manner and consult with a professional.

As far as anxiety is concerned, it's not always a bad thing. It has positive effects too, like it can help you stay focused in the long run, self-motivate you in difficult situations, and even overcome certain challenges because of the adrenaline rush at that period of time. The problem most of the time is when it's in excess in amount and causes malfunction of the body.

How to Check If You have Anxiety or Not?

Are you always in an extremely overwhelmed state of stress, tension, worry, fear, or apprehension?

Are you experiencing some uncanny or uncertain feeling about an event that's going to take place or some unnatural phenomenon?

Are you particularly ritualistic? Do you practice a certain ritual in a certain manner and fear if it is not done in a certain way the result will make you worry or be apprehensive?

Do you experience sudden pain in the chest from nowhere or sweat profusely and panic a lot?

Do you avoid social gatherings and daily activities because of anxiety?

Do you always feel fearful of people, places, and situations?

Well, if you answered yes to any of these questions, then you may be suffering from anxiety.

Well, hold on and don't panic already once you know that you are having anxiety because it is diagnosable and curable too.

Let's go on to understand different types of anxiety disorders.

1. Generalized Anxiety Disorder

If constant worries, fears, or uncanny feelings attack you time and again and manifest in a manner that you're unable to perform your daily activities, then it seems to belong in the category of a generalized anxiety disorder (GAD).

2. Panic/Anxiety Attack

It is associated with a sudden or unexpected and repeated attack of panic as well as experiencing fear oftentimes in different places or situations. In this kind of situation, people tend to avoid public places like shopping malls or confined places like an airplane, social functions, etc.

3. Obsessive Compulsive Disorder (OCD)

In this scenario, people are always known to exhibit irrational behaviors/fears, are very impulsive, repetitive, and stressful, and exacerbate the already existing anxiety. They have the constant feeling of apprehension and superstitious beliefs and may also suffer from obsessively cleaning personal things or items like utensils, rooms, washing hands, checking locks oftentimes, etc.

4. Post-Traumatic Stress Disorder

It's a psychiatric illness that is characterized by a traumatic experience that one had in their lifetime in which, post the experience, they suffer from an associated fear or threat of injury or death of self or someone close to them. It manifests as difficulty in sleeping, concentration, and focus and a feeling of detachment from loved ones.

5. Social Anxiety Disorder

There are people who struggle with social anxiety, which manifests in many different ways, like feeling extremely conscious of self, increased palpitations, profuse sweating, etc. Meeting new people, socializing, and attending events are all places where they're likely to experience more anxiety. It is an extreme feeling of fear and is also quite a common disorder.

6. Special Phobias

We've all heard of different kinds of phobias and even mentioned them to our friends as well. If anyone ever wanted to know what kind of phobias they were suffering from, they'd just pretty much google up the whole thing and use it as a get-to-know-me-better tool too at times. Some of the commonly known phobias include the following:

Agoraphobia: Fear of open spaces

Zoophobia: Fear of animals

Arachnophobia: Fear of spiders

Altophobia: Fear of heights

Aichanophobia: Fear of needles

Commitment Phobia: Fear of commitment

Mycophobia: Fear of germs

Dentophobia: Dental Phobia

The complications of such phobias just worsen the daily life routines. It is seen that alcoholics are ten times more likely to suffer from such phobias when compared to a normal person.

Risk Factors

There is no specific cause as such of these kinds of phobias. The phobia will tend to affect the mental peace of those children whose parents are overprotective and a little too caring. The sufferers of these phobias are more likely to avoid stressful situations or events in life.

The Evil Side of Anxiety

Anxiety, just like people, has a bad side too. Its bad side could probably lead to a lot of problems and pretty much create a huge ruckus in our lives. It might be too much information at this point actually, but bear with me because knowledge is power. Once we know exactly why something happens—the how and the why—we can easily figure out the what and come out from it quickly.

Let's dive into it right away!

Emotional Aspect

As the nature of anxiety is, it's constantly only there to get all the vulnerabilities out of us and pinpoint our flaws. That's how we pretty much feel about this whole setup that it puts us into. To be honest, that's not a wrong description of anxiety, but we have to remember that at all times we're the master of our lives and not our fears.

There are yet some very specific areas that it affects us in our daily lives that I've listed below.

1. **Relationships:** - Anxiety affects all our relationships, especially those who are close to us. It distorts the harmony, interdependency, and interpersonal relationship of the individual to a certain extent. It is specifically unhealthy when socially a lot of people are dependent on you as well.

2. **Motivation:** - Anxiety kills all the motivation that we have. Motivation is the key that drives us all. If not for that accelerator called motivation, I wouldn't have written a book when pharmacy school was just about to end, and you wouldn't be buying this book either. See that?? Now you know a personal secret about me, making us best friends already.

3. **Academic Performance:** - If you don't have a cup of coffee or tea, then get some already. I got a really long rant about this one. Being a paramedic myself, I know how this shit hits bad, like, really bad. The worst part was when I was super anxious before I'd written my pharmacology exam after studying anti-anxiety drugs. It's not too long until the hero himself becomes the villain. Jokes apart, in all seriousness, it causes you to

43

blank out real quick in the exam hall and gives you nightmares that you've never had before, in addition to all the lack of concentration you already have.

4. **Commitment:** A huge term that is often used both in the workplace and in your home, complained about by both your wife and boss. Well, I didn't call out any names, but I guess some did pop, huh?? The bad news, though, is that lack of commitment can put off both people and the universe. This ultimately leads to a dysfunctional life and impedes our growth overall.

Remedies for Anxiety

Since you've read so much already and have quite a good understanding of how anxiety actually works, we can now talk about the different remedies that are in store for all of you. If you've skipped the previous chapter, go read it, and don't cheat this time.

Different groups of people deal with anxiety differently. I'll be giving specific techniques for children, adults, women, teenagers, and the elderly.

Tips for Children

1. **Help your child to identify and feel the feeling:** Guide your children accordingly and help them to identify the different kinds of feelings. Ask them how they feel on a regular basis when encountering different situations. Encourage them to express their feelings to you. Help them to learn different methods of expression like painting, writing, singing, etc. Most importantly, make time for them and listen to them. They're your only hope in a desperate world.

2. **Be a good listener:** You need to initiate this wonderful habit of listening to your child every day. Make it a habit to listen to

your little one for at least 30 minutes after their school is done and encourage them to speak more about their day. Always be proactive, non-judgmental, compassionate, and caring towards them as a listener. Remember that today if you listen, tomorrow they will listen to others and may be a life saver for somebody someday.

3. **Encourage proactive methods:** Engage your children and keep them busy. Encourage and engage them to cope with their anxiety by using different methods that involve kinesthetic learning and movements like dancing, singing, painting, playing the piano, doing some random household chore, playing with mud and bricks, solving puzzles, repeating a tongue twister while doing a specific task, etc.

Tips for Adults

1. **Learn Active Listening Skills:** - Now remember that this is easy. All you have to do is just sit on your balcony, close your eyes, and just listen to everything around you. Start small every day, maybe 5 minutes per day, and then you can exceed the time limit accordingly. When you start listening to nature, you become calm and learn patience. Once you learn that skill, it will be very easy to listen to everyone else around you as well.

2. **Accept Criticism and Rejection:** - Know that criticism and rejection will always be a part and parcel of your life. You aren't an object that is meant to please people around you. Learn to take good and constructive criticism that will actually improve your life by a lot. Rejections are yet another stepping stone to success, so don't feel overwhelmed quickly.

3. **Do Exercises:** When we exercise, we divert our mind and keep ourselves active. Just like the saying goes, "When we look good, we feel good." Exercising not only keeps you in shape

but also releases serotonin and dopamine, which are amazing stress relievers.

Tips for Women

1. **Embrace your Femininity:** The world can be quite a harsh place at times for you to completely acknowledge your feminine traits and even accept them completely. You don't have to worry, though, because there are always people that surround you who help you throughout your journey. Embracing feminism comes in many forms, such as loving yourself, being kind and compassionate, crying your heart out, sending out warmth and acceptance to everyone out there, helping people in need, etc.

2. **Awaken your spiritual powers:** All of us are spiritual beings, but we women are more spiritually active and stronger than men simply because physically they are stronger and more dominant compared to us. Everyone is different in their own spiritual journey. When you decide to take a step further and actually use these spiritual powers to benefit yourself and others to a large extent, you can help the collective consciousness all over the world. You can do this by simply setting the intention to be more spiritual, making a prayer to the God you believe in, and just going about your day as you would. Do not refer to any websites or sources from the internet, for all they have is polluted spirituality. Spirituality is something you learn on your own when nature guides you a certain way. Just stay still and be calm.

Tips for Teenagers

1. **Join Student Community Clubs:** Just fill out a form and join a student club already. Student clubs are a great way to relieve all the excess stress and anxiety that you are going through in

this pupil stage in your life. Sure enough, you have truckloads of assignments, projects, worksheets, and exams ahead, but what makes all of this fun is when you surround yourself with other people who think alike and have the same ideas and aspirations as you too. Let's make this fun for everyone, though a rollercoaster ride still comes with better coping mechanisms that are less narcissistic and more adjusting.

2. **Talk your heart out:** When in trouble, confusion, chaos, or mood swings, just call up a free service counseling center or an NGO that works to cater to the needs of teenagers. If anything is too much to take, don't bother much. Just ring a call and vent it out to any random person. More often the chances are that you feel light and good about yourself, you don't have the fear of getting grounded or your secrets getting revealed, and you have the liberty of setting your emotions free in the way you like.

3. **Travel Frequently**: You can always rely on your parents and ask them to take you on a trip to someplace nearby that you probably never heard of and visit some beaches, hill stations, amusement parks, or even their favorite place, for that matter. Travel with your friends too, but prefer travelling with your parents more often than your friends. Your parents are permanent; everyone else is just temporary.

Tips for the Elderly

1. **Attend Community Prayer Sessions:** In your old age, the best thing to do is live the remaining years of your life happily by dedicating it to the Supreme Divine. By attending community prayer sessions, you not only divert your mind but also meet similar people who are undergoing the same phase as you are currently. Start little by little and have a wonderful reunion with God.

2. **Have a Hobby:** You are almost done with everything you possibly wanted to do, and now is the time you get to focus upon yourself and do something you love. A hobby could be anything from learning how to play a piano, harp, veena, or violin to maybe even learning art, sculpture, painting, makeup, etc.

Chapter 12

Techniques to Improve
Quality of Life

This is the crispiest part and probably the best, I'd say—at least I felt like it when I wrote the book. Maybe you'd disagree with me, and your favorite part would be the one that helped you or resonated the most with your soul as well. I hereby present to you a personal gift from my side that I hope will stay with you forever and help you get through your life's journey.

1. Yoga

This is the most ancient Indian technique, which is a lifesaver and known to be an adjuvant to a more fruitful and healthier living. I personally recommend everyone to do yoga on an everyday basis, as it is very efficient and amazing. I mainly practice the two different kinds of breathing exercises that include Sudarshan Kriya and Pranayama that I was taught in the Art of Living retreat. From my personal experience, I can state that both of these techniques help us to greatly relieve stress, anxiety, and depression and promote positive mental health too.

Sudarshan Kriya

It involves three different paces of breathing one after the other. It starts with slow-paced, medium-paced, and then rapid-paced breathing.

Step 1: Practitioners initially position themselves in Vajrasana, or Diamond pose.

Step 2: Next, they start performing Ujjayi, which requires them to take longer breaths. They are also required to take 2–4 breaths per minute.

Step 3: After the phase Ujjayi is done, they have to perform Bhastrika, which requires them to inhale and exhale air rapidly. It involves taking at least 30 breaths per minute.

Step 4: After this the practitioner chants "OM" consecutively three times.

Note: OM is the sound of the universe and isn't anything religious, but for whatever reason if you feel like not saying it aloud, you can always replace it with Amen or Ameen, which has the same effect.

Pranayama

This is yet another marvelous technique that really helped me get through a lot and, more specifically, this journey as a whole. There are different types of pranayama too. Let's take a look at it.

Type 1: You just sit in a comfortable position and keep inhaling and exhaling with both the nasal passages. This is nothing but quick breathing, which is done at quick intervals in a short span of time.

Type 2: You will have to make use of the Pranava Mudra in here and close the right nostril and inhale through the left nostril and exhale through the same. You can do the same with the left nostril as well and take the right amount of breaths accordingly.

These techniques work phenomenally well. It is drastically known to improve mood, cognition, and intelligence.

2. Yoga Mudras

The mudras used during yoga play an important role as well. These hand gestures activate all the pressure points in our bodies, generating the cure from within. Different mudras have differing properties and uses. They, when used in conjunction during the yoga process, are highly beneficial for the desired purpose you intend for. Mudras yield wonderful results in gaining complete control over the mind and during meditation. The human body is composed of five elements of nature, namely, fire, air, sky, earth, and water. Each of our fingers represents each element. Contact amongst fingers in different patterns brings about balance among the elements, which is the main aim of these mudras. Mudras help in physical, spiritual, and mental upliftment. It enhances both beauty and talent and can be performed regardless of the age and gender of the performer. Always remember that only Gyana, Apana, and Prithvi mudras can be performed every day and not the other mudras. A certain mudra should be performed only till its purpose is served and not beyond that. Let's jump into these mudras one by one.

1. Gyana Mudra

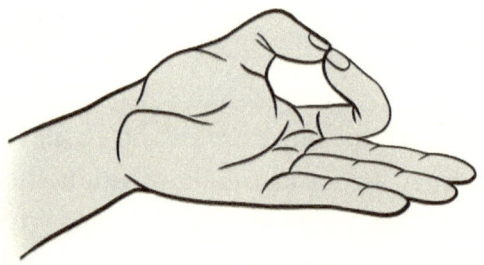

This posture is the most important among all the mudras. I call it the **"King of Mudras."** The reason I call it the King of Mudras is because it mainly affects the pituitary and pineal glands. Gyana mudra can be demonstrated when the tip of the index comes in contact with the thumb. Memory, concentration, and grasping power improve, so students are greatly benefited. Insomnia is cured. All sorts of neurological disorders are greatly benefited by it. Peace of mind is also attained. In addition, the third eye, also known as the pineal gland, gets activated. Hyperactivity and laziness also can be combated by it. This mudra is excellent for children in all aspects, from helping them to learn, concentrate, and memorize to behavior development.

2. Prithvi Mudra

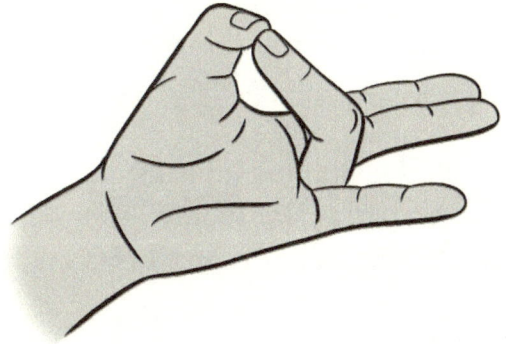

When the tip of the ring finger touches the tip of the thumb, this mudra is demonstrated. It helps to balance the earth element really well. It also helps to enhance beauty, serenity, enthusiasm, and inner glow. It helps you to recharge your inner being and in personality development too. I personally like this mudra very much, as it imparts qualities of tolerance, forgiveness, and balance.

3. Apan Mudra

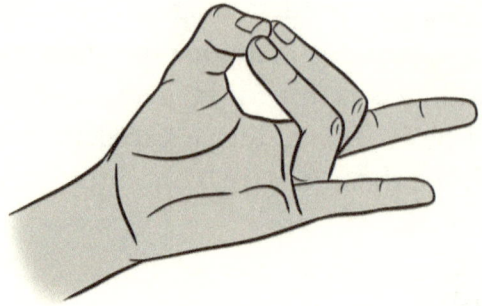

This is demonstrated when the tip of the ring finger and the middle finger come in contact with the tip of the thumb. This mudra is mainly responsible for flushing out the toxic substances from the body. This mudra is specifically advisable for people suffering from diabetes, gastric problems, abdominal pain, and constipation. This mudra could be performed in any posture but is the best in Utkatasana. The functioning of the gastric system improves greatly.

4. Pran Mudra

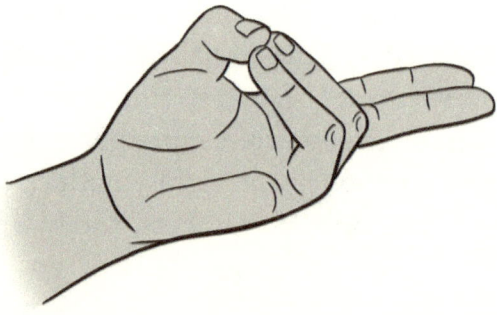

This mudra can be demonstrated when the tips of the ring finger and the little finger touch the tip of the thumb. This mudra improves the circulation of life energy in the body, creating awareness within the performer. It also helps to cure laziness and lethargy by promoting physical health and mental peace. Defects of vision and concentration also greatly improve.

5. Shankh Mudra

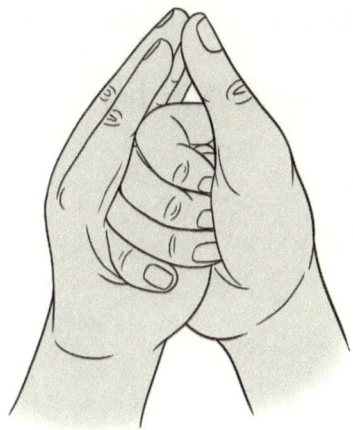

This mudra is demonstrated when the thumb of the left hand is held with the fist of the right, and the tip of the index finger of the left hand touches the tip of the thumb of the right hand. Together the remaining three fingers encircle the right one first, contouring to it with slight pressure. It mainly helps in ailments related to the thyroid and the area around the navel. The Shankh is a symbol of good luck. The blowing of the Shankh symbolizes victory and hence greatly influences the path leading to progress.

6. Dhyan Mudra

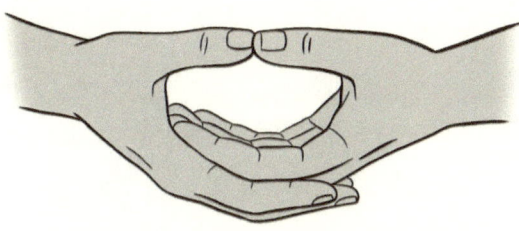

This mudra must be performed while sitting in Padmasana with one hand being placed over the other with the palms facing upwards and the thumbs of both hands touching each other. The performer achieves greater brilliance and becomes an attractive personality by practicing it every day. This mudra greatly helps in improving concentration and influencing people to a significant extent as well.

7. Surabhi/Kamadhenu Mudra

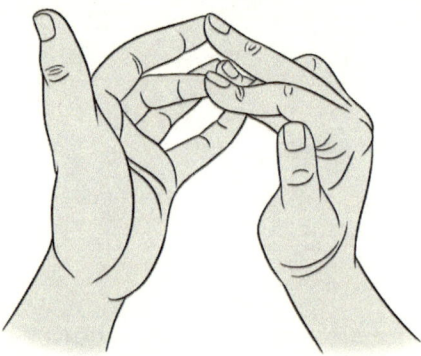

This mudra is demonstrated when the tip of the ring finger of the right hand and the tip of the little finger of the left hand touch each other. The tip of the middle finger of the right hand and the tip of the index finger of the left hand touch each other. The tip of the index finger of the right hand and the tip of the middle finger of the left hand touch each other. The thumb should be held upright. This mudra helps in fulfilling wishes. The performer attains new heights of devotion. It also helps enhance the knowledge. The tridosha, or the triple defect of Vayu, Pitta, and Kapha—that is, gas or acidity—can be easily cured too.

8. Sankalpa Mudra

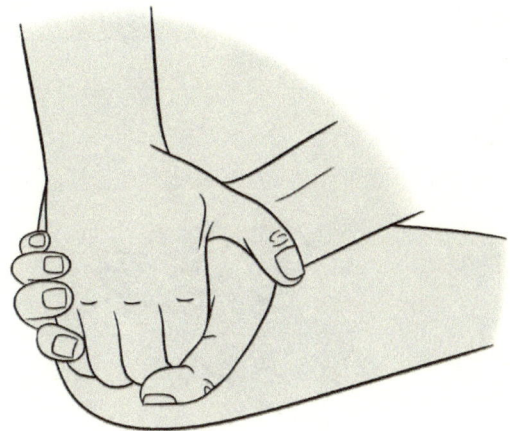

This mudra is demonstrated by placing both the hands on top of the other. When this mudra is performed after having an intention to achieve a particular goal or fulfill a dream, the task becomes easier. This mudra bestows the performer with mental and physical strength, simultaneously instilling in him/her self-confidence and encouragement towards fulfilling his/her wishes.

9. Musal Mudra

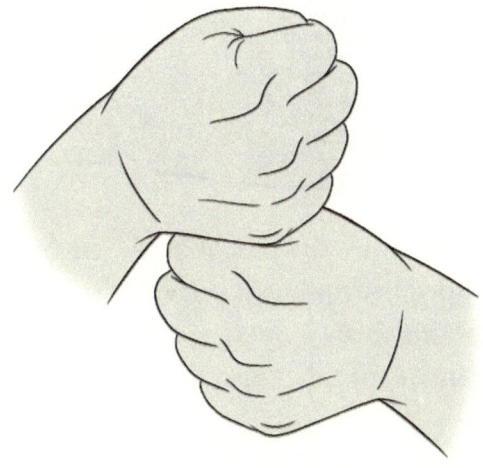

This mudra is demonstrated when the left fist is placed over the right fist. Though it is an effortless mudra to perform, the results are highly effective. It is helpful in overcoming hindrances and problems in life.

10. Kunt Mudra

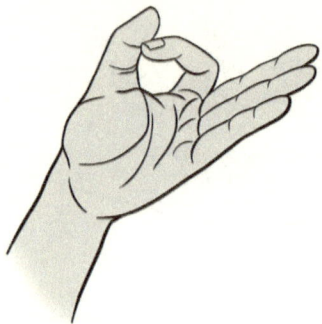

This mudra is demonstrated by holding the index finger upright while the other three fingers remain bent to touch the palm. This mudra helps in protecting you from all kinds of problems.

11. Hamsi Mudra

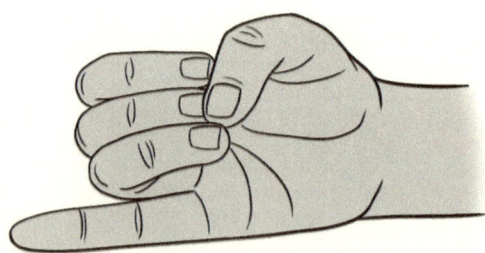

This is demonstrated when the tips of all the fingers except the little finger, which is upright, touch the tip of the thumb. This mudra dispels ignorance and throws open doors towards knowledge. The performer experiences completeness.

12. Anushasan Mudra

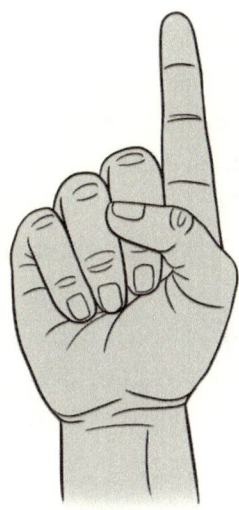

This is demonstrated when the index finger is held upright and the other three fingers bend to touch the palm and are secluded by the thumb. Discipline and leadership qualities can be developed. The performer experiences better work performance and attains an attractive personality.

Note: Everything explained and listed above has been derived from age-old Yogic & Ayurvedic science. All of these observations are purely scientific in nature and not religious, although they could be used for religious purposes in conjunction with other religious elements. When practiced in isolation, they serve more scientific benefits than religious ones.

Manifestation Techniques

Doesn't this thing sound pretty familiar to you? Sure it does, after all those Instagram reels and addictive posts on Instagram. But the real question that lies in here is do you really know these techniques, and are you really using them to their utmost potential? Well, that's on you to find out all these answers......

Let's move on to these techniques.

1. Visual Manifestation Techniques

This is by far the most common technique that has been used widely by most people and is usually taught in psychology classes. The real reason as to why you may be experiencing different results from person to person might be due to the lack of adjuvants used in the process. Using the right kind of adjuvant, like soft soothing music, an open environment, clarity of mind, etc., all play an important role in determining your result. The key to experiencing the best results is not forcing your way into doing things, but simply letting it be. We all need to understand that at different points in our lives we are all in different stages, ranging from a variety of emotions like anger, shallowness, bitterness, jealousy, and lust to happiness, energy, motivation, purpose, and acceptance. We must not lose hold of whatever state we are in currently and strive towards just making our state better through these techniques.

Procedure

1. Make sure that you feel like practicing this technique and not because someone told you to do so.

2. Keep all the distractions aside and immerse yourself in the bounty of nature.

3. Do this in a calm and serene place where the only noise you can hear is that of nature.

4. Now, this is the important deciding factor, so go on reading.

5. There are different kinds of music according to your needs. For example, if your intention is that of cleansing and purifying yourselves, then the sound produced by nature at that instant of time is sufficient. You don't require add-ons.

6. Similarly, if your intention is to attract more wealth, the sound made by coins is what you need to listen to; if love, then the chirping of the birds; if success, then the sound of an uplifting piano piece or drums for that matter.

7. Now once you've identified your need, you can proceed towards the visualization part.

8. Sit in a comfortable position in Vajrasan or Sukhasan and then slowly close your eyes.

9. Just focus on everything around you for the time being and just be attentive of everything around you.

10. Allow yourself to just slip into wherever your subconscious brain wants to go towards.

11. Now slowly, state your intention to your brain and start picturing that scenario or situation that you want to create in your life.

12. Picturize every little detail and feel it coming alive. Nothing is ever impossible, for the word "impossible" tells "I'm possible."

13. Feel the emotions, the energy with that situation, and experience it to the fullest.

14. Now, when you feel like stopping, slowly retract yourself out and let it go slowly.

15. Let go of the imagination, slip into anything else parallelly, and slowly come out through it.

16. Now gently open your eyes and relax for 5 minutes.

17. Let yourself experience the joy and contentment.

18. Be grateful for this joy and express your gratitude in the manner you like.

Note: Do not perform this with anyone else, for your energy may not match with them and might lead to draining more energy if anyone among you has the wrong kind of intentions.

2. Written Technique

This is yet another mind-blowing technique that works out miraculous results. It is mainly based on manifesting or creating your life through the words you believe and write, which creates magic in your life and others' as well when manifested properly. We create our life through the things we speak, write, listen to, and believe, so be wary of these things and make the right call. An important thing to remember while doing this technique is to keep on visualizing the end result or product and write your affirmation with complete belief.

Procedure

1. You may practice this technique with 2 or more people who have a similar intention as yours and who are ready to completely manifest their lives in action.

2. Again, sit in a comfortable position on your chair and take a book and pen and start writing out your affirmation.

3. Make sure you keep a separate book only for your affirmations and don't mix it with anything else.

4. Write down your affirmations for a minimum of 10 times, and the maximum would be anything that you wish.

5. Completely believe that whatever you have written will come true in your life as and when you wish because nothing has fulfilled others' wishes apart from books.

6. Believe in the magic of the books and their power.

7. Relax and chill as your dreams come into your life.

3.Earthing Technique

This is by far my favorite technique. I love this because of its simplicity and the way it can modify itself according to every individual's need. It is highly efficient in cleansing and purifying yourself and the toxic energy you're surrounded by and embedding yourself with positivity. This is the best technique you can use to attract abundance in your life. You can use this to attract anything you want, basically, from your love interest to success in your life.

Procedure

1. Sit in a calm and cool place where you are surrounded by nature, lots of it.

2. Sit on a comfortable chair or a bench and let your feet touch the ground.

3. Let yourself experience the joy when your feet touch the mud and experience the cleansing action of the earth.

4. Just as there are charges present on our body, so are they on the surface of the earth. The earth makes sure to completely drain you of all the negative energy that you've been carrying with you and makes it super positive.

5. Keep observing everything around you and feel the proactiveness in nature.

6. If you feel like sleeping or closing your eyes, feel free to do so and let yourself be.

7. Allow yourself to be in that place for the longest time that is possible for you right now.

8. When you are satisfied enough, get up and get moving and go back to your work.

Reminders to Self

- I am Wonderful.
- I am Amazing.
- I am Love.
- I as much as anyone in the World Deserve Love and to Be Loved.
- I am Pure in Heart.
- I am Kind.
- I am Chaste in Heart.
- I am Forgiving in nature.
- I am Intelligent.
- I am Knowledgeable.
- I am filled with Wisdom of the Holy Spirit.
- I am filled with Goodness.
- I am Meek and Humble in Heart.
- I am Patient.
- I am Generous.
- I am Gracious.
- I am Joyful.
- I am Sacrificing in nature.
- I am Independent.
- I am Able.
- I am Self-Sufficient.
- I am Awesome.
- I am Powerful.
- I am Understanding.

- I am Courageous.
- I am able to Counsel others in need.
- I am Peaceful.
- I am Gentle.
- I am Faithful.
- I am Charismatic.
- I am Modest.
- I am Wealthy.
- I am Successful.
- I am Motivated.
- I am Purposeful.
- I am Magnificent.
- I have Self-Control.
- I am Righteous.
- I am Just.
- I am Protective of myself and others.
- I am Stress-Free.
- I am the constant receiver of Abundance.
- I am Devoted towards God and his purpose in my life.
- I am Compassionate towards all living beings.
- I am Healthy.
- I am Mentally, Physically, Socially and Emotionally Sound.
- I am Virtuous.
- I am Romantic.
- I am Hilarious.
- I am Caring.

- I am Sweet.
- I am Empathetic.
- I am Merciful.
- I am Resourceful.
- I am Unique.
- I am Important.
- I am Strong.
- I am Inspirational.
- I am Beautiful.
- I am Hopeful.
- I am Grateful to everything in my life.
- I am Supportive of others.
- I am the Best.
- I am Proud of Myself.

About the Author

Anisha Roshal Rodrigues is a passionate writer and seeker who believes in the power of self-discovery and authenticity. With a voice that blends honesty, courage, and relatability, she writes to inspire people to embrace their true selves and break free from the noise of societal expectations.

This debut book reflects Anisha's journey of growth, resilience, and reclaiming personal power. It's not just a book, but a conversation with anyone who has ever felt lost, stuck, or unsure of who they are—and a reminder that becoming your realest self is the greatest rebellion.

Beyond writing, Anisha enjoys cooking, learning and exploring conversations that inspire personal growth. Based in Mangalore, she is committed to creating work that sparks reflection, courage, and transformation in readers of all ages.

Follow on:

herkey   @Anisha Roshal Rodrigues

@ahhnisha

@Anisha Rodrigues

@anisharodrigues

@The Anisha Perspective Podcast

@The Anisha Perspective Podcast

Notes

Notes

Notes